Joseph Haydn

Mass in G

No. 7

Joseph Haydn

Mass in G
No. 7

ISBN/EAN: 9783741140365

Manufactured in Europe, USA, Canada, Australia, Japa

Cover: Foto ©Angelika Wolter / pixelio.de

Manufactured and distributed by brebook publishing software
(www.brebook.com)

Joseph Haydn

Mass in G

HAYDN'S

MASS IN G,

(No. 7.)

WITH AN ACCOMPANIMENT FOR THE ORGAN OR PIANO-FORTE.

BY

VINCENT NOVELLO.

WITH LATIN AND ENGLISH TEXT.

BOSTON:
PUBLISHED BY OLIVER DITSON & CO.,
277 WASHINGTON STREET.

HAYDN'S MASS, IN G. (No. 7.)

KYRIE.

Soprano Soli.
Ky - ri - e.... e - lei - - son,
Hear our sup - pli - ca - - tions,

Soprano 2do. Soli.
Ky - ri - e.... e - lei - - son,
Hear our sup - pli - ca - - tions,

Ky - ri - e.... e - lei - son, e - lei - son.
and ac - cept our praise, ac - cept.... our praise.
Chris - -
Je - - -

Ky - ri - e.... e - lei - son, e - lei - son.
and ac - cept our praise, ac - cept.... our praise.
Chris - -
Je - - -

Ky - ri - e.... e - lei - - son,
Hear our sup - pli - ca - - tions,
Chris - -
Je - - -

te, Chris - - te, e - lei - - son, Chris - - te, Christe, e - le - - - i - -
sus, Je - - - sus, our Sa - viour, hear, Je - - sus Christ, ev - er bless - - ed,
te, Chris - - te, e - lei - - son, Chris - - te, e - - lei - - son,
sus, Je - - - sus, our Sav - - iour, Je - - - sus Christ, the bless - ed one,
te, Chris - - - te e - lei - - son, Chris - - te, e - - lei - - son, e
sus, Je - - - - sus, our Sav - - iour, Je - - - sus Christ, the bless - ed one, O,
TUTTI.
son, e - - - lei - - - - - son, e - - - lei - - - son. Chris - - te, Chris-te e -
hear our..... prai - - ses, and ans - wer thou our prayers. Je - - - sus, Christ ev - er
TUTTI.
e - - lei - - son, Christe, e - lei - - son, Chris - - te, Chris-te e - -
hear thou our praises, and ans - wer prayer. Je - - - sus, Christ ev - er
TUTTI.
lei - - son, e - - - - - - - - - lei - - - son Chris - - te, Christe e -
hear.... our prai - - - ses, hear.... our.... prai - - ses, Je - - - sus, Christ ev - er
TUTTI.
lei - - son, e - - lei - - - - son, Christe e - le - i - son, Chris - - te, Chris-te e -
hear.... our prai - - - - - - ses, Je - sus, O hear our prayers, Je - - - sus, Christ ev - er
f
8vi.
8vi.
lei - son, e - lei - - son.
bless - ed, answer thou our prayers.
lei - son, e - lei - son.
bless - ed, answer thou our prayers.
lei - son, e - lei - son.
bless - ed, hear our prayers.
p

SOLI.

Ky - ri - e.... e-lei - - - son, e - lei - - - son.

SOLI. Hear our sup-pli-ca - - - tions, ac - cept our praise.

Ky - ri - e.... e-lei - - son, e - lei - - son,

Hear our sup-pli-ca - - tions, ac - cept our praise,

Ky - ri - e....

Soll. Hear our sup-pli-

Ky - ri - e - ky-ri - e - lei - - son, e - lei -

Hear our sup-pli-ca - - - tions, ac-cept, ac - cept.......... our prais - - - es, and

Ky - ri - e - lei - son, e - - lei-son, e - - lei-son, e -

Hear our sup - pli-ca - - tions, O, hear us, O, hear us, O,

lei - - son, Ky - ri - e - lei - son, e - lei - - -

ca - - tions, Hear our sup-pli-ca - tions, O hear.......... our sup - - - pli-ca - - -

TUTTI.

son, Ky - ri - e - lei - son, e - lei - - -

answer our prayers. Hear our sup-pli-ca - - tions, Ac-cept.......... our prais -

lei - - son, Ky - ri - e - lei - - - son, e - lei-son,

hear us, Hear our sup-pli-ca - - - tions, O hear us,

son, Ky - ri - e - e-lei - son, e - lei - - - -

tions, hear our prayers, Hear our sup-pli-ca - - tions, Ac-cept.......... our

son, Ky - ri - e - e-lei - son, e - lei - - - -

tions, Hear our sup-pli-ca - - tions, Ac-cept.......... our

son, Ky - ri - e e - lei
es, hear us, and ans - wer, our prayers. Hear our sup - pli - ca
e - lei - son, e - lei - son, Ky - ri - e e - lei
O, hear us, O, hear us, Hear our sup - pli - ca
son, e - lei - son, Ky - ri - e e - lei
prais - es, and ans - wer our prayers. Hear our sup - pli - ca
SOLI.
son, Ky - ri - e e - lei - son,
tions, Hear our sup - pli - ca - tions,
SOLI.
son, e - lei - son, e - lei - son,
tions, O, hear us, O, hear us,
son, e - lei - son, e - lei - son,
tions, O, hear us, O, hear us.
SOLI.
p
TUTTI.
Ky - ri - e e - lei - son, e - lei - son, e - lei - son.
Christ, ac - cept our prais - es, ac - cept our prais - es, and ans - wer our prayers.
TUTTI.
Ky - ri - e e - lei - son, e - lei - son, e - lei - son.
Christ, ac - cept our prais - es, ac - cept our praise, and ans - wer our prayers.
TUTTI.
Ky - ri - e e - lei - son, e - lei - son, e - lei - son.
Christ, ac - cept our prais - es, ac - cept our praise, and ans - wer prayers.
TUTTI.
f

GLORIA.

Te, be - ne - di - cimus Te,
Lord, praise and bless ye his name,
Lau - damus Te, be - ne - di - cimus Te,
O praise the Lord, praise and bless ye his name,
Lau - damus Te, be - ne - di - cimus Te,
O praise the Lord, praise and bless ye his name,
Laudamus Te, be - ne -
O praise the Lord, praise and
a - do-ramus Te a - do - ramus Te, glo - ri - fi - camus Te, glo - ri - fi -
praise and bless the Lord, and adore his name, and glo - ri - fy ye him, and glo - ri -
a - do - ra-mus Te, a - do - ramus Te, glo - ri - fi - camus Te, glo - ri - fi -
praise and bless the Lord, and adore his name, and glo - ri - fy ye him, and glo - ri -
a - do - ra-mus Te, a - do - ramus Te, Glo - ri - fi - camus Te,
praise and bless the Lord, and adore his name, And glo - ri - fy ye him.
di - ci - mus, a - do - ramus Te, Glo - ri - fi - camus Te,
bless his name, and adore his name, And glo - ri - fy ye him,
8vi. 8vi.
camus Te, glo - ri - fi - ca - mus Te, glo - ri - fi - ca - mus Te: Te, Te lau -
fy ye him, and glo - ri - fy ye him, and glo - ri - fy ye him: Thou art ex -
camus Te, glo - ri - fi - ca - mus Te, glo - ri - fi - ca - mus Te: Te, Te lau -
fy ye him, and glo - ri - fy ye him, and glo - ri - fy ye him: Thou art ex -
glo - ri - fi - camus Te, glo - ri - fi - ca - mus Te: Te, Te lau -
and glo - ri - fy ye him, and glo - ri - fy ye him: Thou art ex -

da - mus, be - ne - di - ci - mus a - do - ramus,   Glo - ri - fi - ca -
alt - ed, art ex - alt - ed above the heavens,   We praise and glo - - - -

da - mus, be - ne - di - ci - mus a - do - ramus,   glo - ri - fi - ca -
alt - ed, art ex - alt - ed above the heavens,   we praise and bless

da - mus, be - ne - di - ci - mus, a - do - ramus,   glo - ri - fi - ca -
alt - ed, art ex - alt - ed above the heavens,   we praise and bless

- mus Te, glo - ri - fi - ca - mus Te,   Gloria in ex - cel - sis,   De - o!
- ri - fy Thee, we praise and bless thy name,   Glory in the highest,   glo - ry!

mus, glo - ri - fi - ca - - - mus Te,   Gloria in ex - cel - sis,   De - o!
thee, we glo - ri - fy thy name,   Glory in the highest,   glo - ry!

- mus, Te glo - ri - fi - ca - mus Te,   Gloria in ex - cel - sis,   De - o!
thee, glo - ri - fy and bless thy name,   Glory in the highest,   glo - ry!

magnam glo — ri — am tu — am, propter magnam, magnam glo-ri-am
mer — cy, great............... thy glo-ry, great thy praise shall be, thy glo-ry thro'

tu — am: Do-mi-ne, Do-mi-ne De-us Rex Cœ-les-tis!
end — less years: Praise ye the Lord ev-er-last-ing, praise ye the Lord!

De — us Pa — ter om-ni-po-tens, Do — mi-ne
praise the Fa — ther om-ni-po-tent, praise............ ye the

Fi — li — u-ni ge-ni-te, u-ni ge-ni-te, Je —
Son di-vine, the on-ly Son, praise ye the Son di-vine, Je —

su, Je — su Christe. Do-mi-ne, Do-mi-ne De-us, ag — nus
sus, Je — sus, Saviour, Son of the Father, and Lamb of God, Son of the

De - i, Fi - lius, Pa - tris, Fi - lius, Fi - li - us Pa -
Fa - ther, Je - sus, Sav - iour, Je - sus, Son of the Fa -

TUTTI.

- tris. pec - ca - ta mun - di.
- ther. a - way transgress - ion.

TUTTI.
pec - ca - ta mun - di.
a - way transgress - ion.

TUTTI.
pec - ca - ta mun - di.
a - way transgress - ion.

TUTTI
Qui tol - - - lis pec - ca - ta mun - di.
Who tak - - eth a - way transgress - ion.

8vi.

SOLI.
Mi - se - re - re no - - - bis.
Mer - cy show un - to........ us.
SOLI.
Mi - se - re - re no - - - bis.
Mer - cy show un - to us.
SOLI.
Mi - se - re - re no - - bis.
Mer - cy show un - to us.
SOLI.
Mi - se - re - re no - - bis. TUTTI.
Mer - cy show un - to us. Qui tol - - -
Thou who tak - - -

pec - ca - ta mundi, sus - ci - pe de - pre - ca - ti - o - nem
a - way transgression, Thou who dost plead for us be - fore the

pec - ca - ta mundi, sus - ci - pe de - pre - ca - ti - o - nem
a - way transgression, Thou who dost plead for us be - fore the

pec - ca - ta mundi, sus - ci - pe de - pre - ca - ti - o - nem
a - way transgression, Thou who dost plead for us be - fore the

lis pec - ca - ta mundi, sus - ci - pe de - pre - ca - ti - o - nem
est a - way transgression, Thou who dost plead for us be - fore the

nos - tram, sus - ci - pe, Qui se - des ad dex - tram
Fa - ther, par - don us, Thou at the right hand of

nos - tram, sus - ci - pe, Qui se - des ad dex - tram
Fa - ther, par - don us, Thou at the right hand of

nos - tram, sus - ci - pe, Qui se - des ad dex - tram
Fa - ther, par - don us, Thou at the right hand of

100 = ♩ Allegro. TUTTI.
Quo - ni - am tu so - - - lus sanc - tus tu so - - - lus
For thou on - ly, for thou on - ly art ho - - - ly,
TUTTI.
Quo - ni - am tu so - - lus sanc - tus tu so - lus
For thou on - ly, for thou on - ly art ho - ly,
TUTTI.
Quo - ni - am tu so - lus sanc - tus tu so - lus
For thou on - ly, for thou on - ly art ho - ly,
TUTTI.
Quo - ni - am tu so - - lus sanc - tus tu so - lus
For thou on - ly, for............ thou on - ly art ho - ly,
Allegro.
Full without Trumpet.
8vi.
Do - mi-nus tu so - lus al - tis - si - mus, Je - su Chris - te, Cum sancto
For thou on - ly reign - est with God on high, Je - sus Christ the Lord, Thou with the
Do - mi-nus tu so - lus al - tis - si - mus, Je - su Chris - te, Cum sancto
For thou on - ly reign - est with God on high, Je - sus Christ the Lord, Thou with the
Do - mi - nus tu so - lus al - tis - si - mus, Je - su Chris - te, Cum sancto
For thou on - ly reign - est with God on high, Je - sus Christ the Lord, Thou with the
Do - mi-nus tu so - lus al - tis - si - mus, Je - su Chris - te, Cum sancto
For thou on - ly reign - est with God on high, Je - sus Christ the Lord, Thou with the
spi - ri - tu in glo - ria De - i Pa - tris; A - men, A - - men.
Ho - ly Spir-it in the Father's glo - ry; A - men, A - - men.
spi - ri - tu in glo - ria De - i Pa - tris; A - men, A - - men.
Ho - ly Spir-it in the Father's glo - ry; A - men, A - - men.
spi - ri - tu in glo - ria De - i Pa - tris; A - men, A - - men.
Ho - ly Spir-it in the Father's glo - ry; A - men, A - - men.

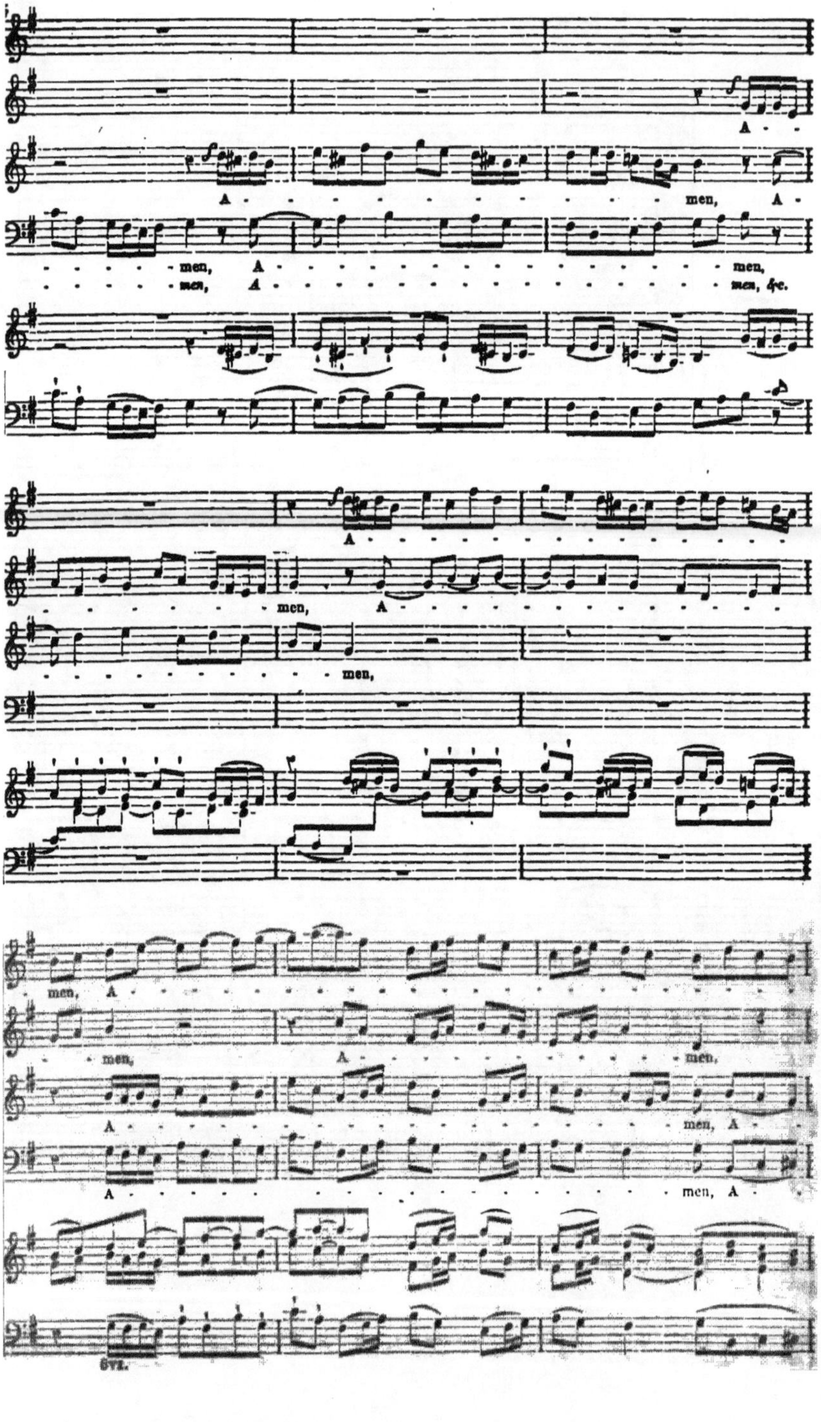
A - men, A -
men, A - men,
men, &c.
A - men,
men,
men, A -
men, A -
men,
A - men, A -
A - men, A -
8va.

men, A - - - - - - - - - - - - men, A - - - -
A - - - - - - men, A - - - - -
men, A - - - - - - - - - - - - men,
men, A - - - - - - - - - men, A - - - - -
Ped.
- - - - - - - - - - - - men, A - - - men, A - - -
- - - - - - - - - - - - men, A - - - men, A - - -
A - - - - - - - - - - - men, A - - - men, A - - - -
- - - - - - men, A - men. A - - - men, A -
8vi.

CREDO.

112 = ♩ *Allegro.* TUTTI.

Cre - do in u - num De - um, Pa - trem om - ni - po - ten - tem fac
I be - lieve in God the Fa - ther, God of an in - fi - nite ma - jes

TUTTI.
Cre - do, Cre - do, ge - ni - tum non fac - tum,
God the Fa - ther, reign - ing un - cre - a - ted,

TUTTI.
Cre - do, Cre - do, De - um do De - o,
God the Fa - ther, God o - ver all things,

TUTTI.
Et in u - num Do - mi - num Je - sum Chris - tum,
In one Lord on - ly, Je - sus Christ the Sav - iour,

Allegro.
Full to 15.

to - rem Cœ - li et ter - ræ,
ty, Cre - a - tor of heav'n and earth,

con - sub - stan - ti - a - lem Pa - tri,
power - ful in the heavens still dwell - ing,

lu - men de lu - mi - ne, De - um ve - rum,
source of all light and truth, Lord of all things,

Fi - li - um De - um - ni - ge - ni - tum,
Son of the High - est, on - ly Son of God,

vi - si - bi - li - um, et in vi - si - bi - li - um, et in
Who en - light - en - eth, yet who dwells in - vi - si - ble, yet who

per quem om - ni - a per quem om - ni - a, fac
and by him were all things in heaven and on earth.....

De - um ve - rum de De - o ve - ro, De - um
true and on - ly God, God the Fa - ther, true and

et ex Pa - tre, ex Pa - tre na - tum, an - te
Son of God, the Son of the Fa - ther, In to

vi - si - bi - li - um, qui propter nos ho - mi - nes et
dwells in vis - i - ble, who of his great mer - cy came from

in, fac - ta sunt, qui propter nos ho - mi - nes et
cre - a - ted, who of his great mer - cy came from

ve - rum de De - o ve - - - ro, qui propter nos ho - mi - nes et
on - ly God, God the Fa - - ther, who of his great mer - cy came from

om - ni - a sæ - - cu - la, qui propter nos ho - mi - nes et
Sa - viour Je - - sus Christ, who of his great mer - cy came from

prop - ter nos - tram sa - lu - tem des - cen - dit, de Cœ - lis des -
heaven, de - scend - ed, de - scend - ed from heaven, who de - scend - ed from

prop - ter nos - tram sa - lu - tem des - cen - dit, des - cen -
heaven, de - scend - ed, de - scend - ed from heaven, who de - scend -

prop - ter nos - tram sa - lu - tem des - cen - dit, des - cen - dit, des -
heaven, de - scend - ed, de - scend - ed from heaven, who de - scend - ed from

66 = ♪
Adagio. QUARTETTO.*
TENOR SOLO.
TENOR.
Et in-car-na-tus est de spi - - ri-tu sanc-to, Et in-car-na-tus est de
Who was in Be'lem born, as-sum'd our mortal state, He in hu-mil-i-ty as-
Swell. 2 Diaps.
Adagio.
tenuto
Dulciana.
spi - - ri - tu sancto ex Ma-ri-a, Ma-ri-a Vir-gi-ne et Ho-mo, et
sumed our mor-tal state. Son of the vir-gin Ma-ry, he be-came a mor-tal, in
tr
Ho - - - mo fac - - - tus est et Ho-mo et Ho - - mo fac - tus
hu - - - - man form....... ap-peared, the Saviour as man ap - - peared,....
SOLO.
Cru-ci-fix-us e-ti-am
That he might be cru-ci-fied,
SOLO.
Cru-ci-fix-us e-ti-am pro no - bis
That he might be cru-ci-fied, to save us,
SOLO.
Cru-ci-fix-us e-ti-am pro no - bis sub Pon-ti-o Pi-
That he might be crucified, to save us, he, un-der Pontius
et Ho-mo fac - tus est et Ho-mo fac-tus est
in hu-man form appeared, a mortal he became,
Cru-ci-fix-us e-ti-am pro no-bis sub Pon-ti-o Pi-la-to pas-sus pas-sus
that he might be cru-ci-fied, to save us, he, un-der Pontius Pilate, suf-fered, suffered

mor - tu - os cu - jus reg - ni non e - rit fi - nis et u - nam
quick and the dead. His king - dom shall be for - ev - er with all the

mor - tu - os cu - jus reg - ni non e - rit fi - nis et u - nam
quick and the dead. His king - dom shall be for - ev - er with all the

Fi - li - o si - mul a - do - ra - tur et con - glo - ri - fi - ca - tur et u - nam
quick and the dead. Come glo - ri - fy him, he reign - eth for - ev - er with all the

o - que pro - ce - dit qui lo - cu - tus est per.......... Pro - phe - tas et u - nam
Fa - ther, as hath been pro-phe-sied by the ho - - ly proph - ets, with all the

sanc - tam ca - tho - li - cam et a - pos - to - li - cam Ec - cle - si - am con - fi - te - or u - nam bap -
church, with all saints and ho - ly men of an - cient time, with all the migh - ty, glo - rious host of his re -

sanc - tam ca - tho - li - cam et a - pos - to - li - cam Ec - cle - si - am con - fi - te - or u - nam bap -
church, with all saints and ho - ly men of an - cient time, with all the migh - ty, glo - rious host of his re -

sanc - tam ca - tho - li - cam et a - pos - to - li - cam Ec - cle - si - am con - fi - te - or u - nam bap -
church, with all saints and ho - ly men of an - cient time, with all the migh - ty, glo - rious host of his re -

Svi.

tis - ma in re - mis - si - o - nem pec - ca - to - rum et ex - pec - to re - sur - rec - ti - o - nem mor -
deem'd ones. They, with him, shall reign in bliss for - ev - er, in the res - ur - rec - tion they shall reign with him

tis - ma in re - mis - si - o - nem pec - ca - to - rum et ex - pec - to re - sur - rec - ti - o - nem mor -
deem'd ones. They, with him, shall reign in bliss for - ev - er, in the res - ur - rec - tion they shall reign with him

tis - ma in re - mis - si - o - nem pec - ca - to - rum et ex - pec - to re - sur - rec - ti - o - nem mor -
deem'd ones. They, with him, shall reign in bliss for - ev - er, in the res - ur - rec - tion they shall reign with him

ff
tu - o - - - - rum et vi - tam ven - tu - - ri sæ - - cu - li A - - - -
ev - er - - - - more, they all shall be with him ev - - er-more, A - - - -
ff
tu - o - - - - rum et vi - tam ven - tu - - ri sæ - - cu - li A - - - -
ev - er - - - - more, they all shall be with him ev - - - er-more, A - - - -
ff
tu - o - - - - rum et vi - tam ven - tu - - ri sæ - cu - li A - - - -
ev - er - - - - more, they all shall be with him ev - - er - more, A - - - -
ff
tu - o - - - - rum et vi - tam ven - tu - - ri sæ - cu - li A - men,
ev - er - - - - more, they all shall be with him ev - er - more, A - men,
FULL
- - - - - - - men, A - - - - men, A - - - - men, A
A - - - - - - men, A - - - - men, A - - - - - - men, A -
- - - - - - - men, A - - - - men, A - - - - - - men, A -
A - men, A - men, A - - - - men, A - - - - men, A -
tr
8vi.
- - - men, A - - - - - - - men, A - - - - men, A - men.
- - - men, A - - - - men, A - - - - men, A - men.
- - - men, A - - - - - - men, A - - - - men, A - men.
- - - men, A - - - - - men, A - - men, A - - - - men, A - men.
tr

sub Pon-ti-o Pi-la-to pro no-bis pas-sus et se-pul-tus
He, un-der Pontius Pilate, to save us, suf-fered, and was bu-ried.
la-to pas-sus et se-pul-tus
Pi-late, in... the... sep-ul-chre was
Cru-ci-fix-us etiam pas-sus et se-pul-tus e-ti-am pro
cru-ci-fied, to save us, died,... and in the se-pul-chre was laid, to
et se-pul-tus est sub Pon-ti-o Pi-la-to pas-sus et se-pul-tus
He, to.... save us, died. He, un-der Pontius Pi-late, suf-fered, in the grave was
est pro-no-bis pas-sus et se-pul-tus est pas-sus, pas-sus et se-pul-tus
He, to save us, died,.... and in the sep-ul-chre was laid, in...... the sep-ul-chre was
est.... pro no-bis sub Pon-ti-o Pi-la-to pas-sus pas-sus et se-pul-tus
laid.. To save us, he, un-der Pontius Pi-late, suf-fered, in the sep-ul-chre was
cres.
no-bis pas-sus, pas-sus, pas-sus et se-pul-tus
save us, died..................... He suf-fered, in the sep-ul-chre was
est pro-no-bis pas-sus est pas-sus, pas-sus pro-
laid, to save us, cru-ci-fied, suf-fered, bu-ried, to
p pp
est pro no-bis sub Pon-ti-o se-pul-tus est.
laid, to save us, was cru-ci-fied, was cru-ci-fied.
est et se-pul-tus pas-sus et se-pul-tus, se-pul-tus est.
laid, he was bu-ried, suf-fered, and was bu-ried, was cru-ci-fied.
est Cru-ci-fix-us pas-sus et se-pul-tus, se-pul-tus est.
no-bis sub Pon-ti-o Pi-la-to se-pul-tus est.
save us, was cru-ci-fied, was bu-ried, was cru-ci-fied.

Allegro.
TUTTI.

Et re - sur - rex - it ter - ti - a di - e se - cun-dum scrip-tu - ras et as - cen - dit in
On the third day he rose a - gain, rose, that the scripture might be ful-filled, as - cend - ed to

TUTTI.

Et re - sur - rex - it ter - ti - a di - e se - cun-dum scrip-tu - ras et as - cen - dit in
On the third day he rose a - gain, rose, that the scripture might be ful-filled, as - cend - ed to

TUTTI.

Et re - sur - rex - it ter - ti - a di - e se - cun-dum scrip-tu - ras et as - cen - dit in
On the third day he rose a - gain, rose, that the scripture might be ful-filled, as - cend - ed to

TUTTI.

Allegro.   f Full to 15.

8vi.

Cœ - lum se - det ad dex - te - ram Pa - - - - - tris et i - te - rum ven-
heaven, at the right hand of the Fa - - - - - ther he reign - eth, and from

Cœ - lum se - det ad dex - te - ram Pa - - - - - tris et i - te - rum ven-
heaven, at the right hand of the Fa - - - - - ther he reign - eth, and from

Cœ - lum se - det ad dex - te - ram Pa - - - - - tris et i -
heaven, at the right hand of the Fa - - - - - ther, with the

Allegro. 116 =
TUTTI. f
Ple - ni sunt Cœ - - - li et ter - - - ra
All things in heaven and on earth
Glo - ri - a tu - a glo - ri - a glo - ri - a glo - ri - a tu - a
tell of thy glo - ry, tell of thy ma - jes - ty, and thy great glo - ry.
Allegro.
Full, with Trumpet.
8vi.
Ho - san - na in ex - cel - - - sis in.... ex - cel - - sis Ho -
Ho - san - na in the high - - - est, in.... the high - - est, Ho -
Ho - san - - - na in.... ex - cel - - sis Ho
Ho - san - - - na in.... the high - - est, Ho
p

san - na in ex - cel - - - - - sis, in ex - - cel - - sis.
san - na in the high - - - - - - est, in the high - - - - est.

san - na in ex - cel - - - - - sis, in ex - - cel - - sis.
san - na in the high - - - - - - est, in the high - - - - est.

san - na in ex - cel - - sis, in ex - - cel - - sis.
san - na in the high - - - est, in the high - - - - est.

san - - - - - - na in ex - - cel - - sis.
san - - - - - - na in the high - - - est.

BENEDICTUS.

88 = ♩ QUARTETTO.
Swell. 2 Diaps. & Pris.

Moderato.

Dulciana.

SOLO.

Be - ne - dic - tus qui ve - nit qui ve - nit
Bless - ed, bless - ed is he who cometh, aye,

SOLI.
in aye,

in aye,
SOLI.

Sw: 2 Diapasons.

Swi.

SANCTUS.

66 = ♪
Swell Hautboy.
p
Choir Dulciana.
Adagio.
TUTTI.
Sanc - tus, sanc - tus, sanc - tus,
Ho - ly, ho - ly, ho - ly.

Sanc - tus, Dominus De - us Sa - baoth,
Ho - ly, ho-ly Lord God of Sab - aoth,
Sanc - tus Do - minus De - us Sa - baoth, Dominus De - us Sa - - - baoth.
Ho - ly, ho - ly Lord God of Sab - a-oth, holy Lord God of Sab - - - aoth,
Full to 15.
Sanc - tus Dominus De - us Sa - ba - oth, Sa - - ba -
Ho - ly, holy Lord God of Sab - a - oth, Sab - - - a -
Sanc - tus Dominus De - us Sa - baoth, Dominus De - us, De - us Sa - ba
Ho - ly, holy Lord God of Sab - aoth, holy Lord God of Sab - aoth, Sab - - a -
Dominus Deus Sa - - ba - oth, Dominus De - us Sa - - - - ba -
Holy Lord God of Sab - - a - oth, holy Lord God of Sab - - - - a -
Sanc - tus Dominus Deus Sa - - - - ba-oth, Sa - ba -
Ho - ly, holy Lord God of Sab - - - a - oth, Sab - a -
oth, Sanc - - tus, Sanc - - tus.
oth, Ho - - ly, Ho - - ly.
oth, Sanc - - tus, Sanc - - tus.
oth, Ho - - ly, Ho - - ly.
oth, Sanc - - tus, Sanc - - tus.
oth, Ho - - ly, Ho - - ly.
oth, Sanc - - tus, Sanc - - tus.
oth, Ho - - ly, Ho - - ly.

dolce.
Be - - ne - dic - tus qui
Bless - - ed, Blessed is
no - mi - ne in no - mi - ne in no - mi - ne Do - - mi - ni
bless - ed is he.... who com - eth in the name of...... the Lord.
no - mi - ne in no - mi - ne in no - mi - ne Do - - mi - ni
bless - ed is he.... who com - eth in the name of...... the Lord.
no - - mi - ne Do - mi - ni in no - mi - ne Do - mi - ni
bless - ed is he who com - eth in...... the name of the Lord.
cres.
ve - nit qui ve - nit in no - - - mi - ne in no - - - - - - mi - ne in no - mine Do - mi - ni
he.... who com - eth, aye, bless - ed who cometh, bless - - - ed who com - eth in.. the name of the Lord,
cres. in no - - - mi - ne in no - - - - - - mi - ne in nomine Do - mi - ni
aye, bless - ed who cometh, bless - - - ed who cometh in.. the name of the Lord,
cres. in no - - - mi - ne in no - - - - - - mi - ne in nomine Do - mi - ni qui
aye, bless - ed who cometh, bless - - - ed who cometh in.. the name of the Lord, who
Be - ne - dic - tus qui ve - nit in no - mi - ne no - mine Do - mi - ni
he is bless - ed who comes in the name of the Lord, in the name of the Lord,
Be - ne - dic - - - tus qui ve - nit in no - - mi - ne Do - - - - -
he is bless - - - ed, who com - eth in.... the name of
Be - ne - dic - - - tus qui ve - nit in no - mi - ne in no - - - - - -
Bless - ed, bless - - - ed, who comes in the name of the Lord.
ve - - - - - - nit in no - - - - mi - ne no - - mi - ne Do - - -
comes in the name of the Lord, in the name..............
Be - ne - dic - tus qui ve - nit in no - - -
He is bless - ed, who cometh in the..............

mi-ni in no-mine Do-mi-ni
Be-ne-dic-tus qui
the Lord, who com-eth in the name of the Lord;
He is bless-ed, who
mi-ne in no-mi-ne Do-mi-ni
Be-ne-
the Lord, who com-eth in the name of the Lord;
Bless-ed,
mi-ni in no-mi-ne Do-mi-ni
Be-ne-dic-tus qui
of the Lord, who com-eth in the name of the Lord;
He is bless-ed, who
mi-ne in no-mi-ne Do-mi-ni
name of the Lord, in the name of the Lord;
ve-nit qui ve-nit in no-mi-ne no-mi-ne Do-mi-ni
com-eth, who comes in the name of the Lord in the name of the Lord.
dic-tus qui ve-nit in no-mi-ne no-mi-ne Do-mi-ni
bless-ed who comes in the name of the Lord, in the name of the Lord.
ve-nit qui ve-nit in no-mi-ne Do-mi-ni
com-eth, who comes in the name in the name of the Lord.
in no-mi-ne no-mi-ne Do-mi-ni
who comes in the name in the name of the Lord.
tr
mf Gt. Diaps.
8vi.
tr

dolce.
Be-ne-dic-tus qui ve-nit
He is bless-ed, who com-eth,
Be - ne-dic-tus qui ve-nit qui ve-nit Be-ne-dic-tus qui ve-nit
Bless - ed, bless-ed be he.... who com-eth, He is bless-ed, who com-eth,
Be-ne-dic-tus qui ve-nit
He is bless-ed, who com-eth
Be-ne-dic - - - - - - tus qui ve - - - - - - nit in
Blessed, bless - - - - - - ed be he.................. who
8vi. 8vi. 8vi.
in no-mi-ne Do - - - - - - - - mi-ni Be - - ne-dic-tus qui ve-nit qui ve-nit
blessed, he who com - - - - - - - eth in the name of the Lord; who com-eth, who com-eth,
in no-mi-ne Do - - - - - - - - - - - mini Be - - ne-dic-tus qui ve - nit qui ve - nit
blessed, he who com - - - - - - eth in the name of the Lord; who com - eth, who com-eth,
in no-mi-ne Do - - - - - - - - - - mi-ni Be - - ne-dic - tus qui ve - nit qui ve-nit
blessed, he who com - - eth, ... in the name, who com - eth, who com - eth, who com-eth,
no - mi ne Do - - - - - - - - - - - mini Be - ne-dic - tus qui ve - nit qui ve - nit
comes in the name...................... of the Lord, who com - eth, who com - eth, who com - eth,
Be - ne-dic-tus qui ve-nit Bene-dic - tus
Bless - ed, bless-ed, who com-eth, he is bless - ed,
Be - ne-dic-tus qui ve-nit in no - - - - -
Bless - ed, bless-ed, who com-eth in the name..............................
Be - - - ne-dic-tus Be-ne-dic-tus qui ve-nit Be-ne-dic - tus
com - - eth, who com - eth in the name, who com-eth, bless-ed, bless - ed,
Be - ne-dic-tus qui ve-nit Benedic-tus
Bless - ed, bless-ed, who com-eth, he is blessed,

qui ve - nit in no - - mi - ne Do - - - - - - - - -
is bless - ed who com - eth in the name
- - - - mi - ne Do - mi - ni in no - - - - - - - -
of the Lord, who com - eth in
qui ve - nit in no - mi - ne in no - - mi - ne Do - - - - - - - -
who com - eth, who com - eth in the name of the Lord, bless - - - - - ed, who
qui ve - nit in no - - - - - - - - mi - ne
who com - eth in the name of the
8va.
cres.
- - - mi - ni in no mine Do - mi - ni Be - - - - - ne - dic - - -
who com - eth in .... the name of the Lord, Bless - - - - - - ed, bless
cres.
- - - mi - ne in no - mine Do - mi - ni Be - ne - dic - tus qui ve - nit qui ve - nit in
the name, the name, the name of the Lord, He is bless - ed, is bless - ed, who comes in the
- - mi - ni in no - mine Do - mi - ni Be - ne - dic - tus qui ve - nit qui ve - nit in
comes in the name, in the name of the Lord, He is bless - ed, is bless - ed, who comes in the
Do - mi - ni in no - mine Do - mi - ni qui ve - nit in
Lord, who comes in the name of the Lord, who com - eth, who
cres.
tus qui ve - - - nit in no - mi - ne Do - - - mi - ni in no - mi - ne Do - - mi -
ed who com - - - eth, who comes in the name of the Lord, the name of the
no - - - - - - - - - mi - ne Do - - mi - - ni in no - mi - ne Do - - - mi -
name, in the name, the name, the name of the
no - - - - - - - mi - ne Do - - - - mi - ni in no - mi - ne Do - - - mi
name, in the name, the name, the name of the
no - - - - - - - - - mi - ne Do - - - mi - ni in no - mi - ne Do - mi - - -
com - eth in the name of the Lord, the name, the name of the

ni.
Lord.
116 = ♩ Allegro.
TUTTI.
Ho - san - - na in.... ex - cel - - - - - - - - sis
Ho - san - - na in.... the high - - - - - - - - - est,
Allegro.
Full.
in.... ex - cel - - - - sis
in.... the high - - - - est,
Ho - san - - na in.... ex - cel - - - - - -
Ho - san - - na in.... the high - - - - - -
Ho - san - - - - - - - - - - - -
Ho - san - - - - - - - - - - - -

AGNUS DEI.

re - - re mi - - se - re - - re no - - - bis
God, for - give, have mer - - cy on - - - us.

re - - re mi - - se - re - - re no - - - bis
God, for - give, have mer - - cy on........ us.

re - - re mi - - se - re - - re no - - - bis
God, for - give, have mer - - cy on............ us.

Ag - - nus De - i qui tol - lis pec - ca - ta
Lamb of God,.. who ta - kest a - way the

Ag - - nus De - i qui tol - lis pec - ca - ta
Lamb of God,.. who ta - kest a - way the

Ag - - nus De - i qui tol - lis pec - ca - ta
Lamb of God,.. who ta - kest a - way the

mun - di pec - ca - ta mun - di mi - se - re - re mi - - se - re - - re
sins of the world, have mer - cy, Lamb of God, have mer - - cy on - us,

mun - di pec - ca - ta mun - di mi - se - re - re mi - - se - re - - re
sins of the world, have mer - cy, Lamb of God, have mer - - cy on - us,

mun - di pec - ca - ta mun - di mi - se - re - re mi - - se - re - - re
sins of the world, have mer - cy, Lamb of God, have mer - - cy on - us,

mi - se - re - - re, mi - se - re - - re no - - - - bis.
Lamb of God, for - give, have mer - - cy on - - - - - - - - us.

mi - se - re - - re, mi - se - re - - re no - - - - bis.
Lamb of God, for - give, have mer - cy on - - - - - us.

mi - se - re - - re, mi - se - re - - re no - - - - bis.
Lamb of God, for - give, have mer - cy on - - - - - us.

mf
Ag - - nus De - i qui tol - lis, qui
Lamb of God, who ta - kest, who

mf
Ag - - nus De - i qui tol - lis, qui
Lamb of God, who ta - kest, who

mf
Ag - - nus De - i, qui tol - lis, qui
Lamb of God, who ta - kest, who

mf
tr
mf

tol - lis pec - ca - ta mun - di pec - ca - - ta mun - di.
ta - kest a - way the sins of the world, have mer - cy.

tol - lis pec - ca - ta mun - di pec - ca - - ta mun - di.
ta - kest a - way the sins of the world, ... have mer - cy.

tol - lis pec - ca - ta mun - di pec - ca - - ta mun - di.
ta - kest a - way the sins of the world, have mer - cy.

112 = ♩ *Allegretto.*

Swell 2 Diaps.

Allegretto.

p

SOLI.

Do - na no - bis pa - cem,
Lord, thy mer - cies still increase,

SOLI.

Do - na no - bis pa - cem,
Lord, thy mer - cies still increase,

tr   *tr*

mez: f   *p*

8vi.

Do - na no - bis, no - bis pa - - cem,   Do -
Give us, give us, Lord, en - dur - ing peace,   *Give*

Do - na no - bis, no - bis pa - - cem,   Do -
Give us, give us, Lord, en - dur - ing peace,   *Give*

SOLI.

Do - na no - bis pa - - cem,   Do -
Lord, thy mer - cies still increase,   *Give*

SOLI.

Do - na no - bis pa - - cem,   Do
Lord, thy mer - cies still increase,   *Give*

-na, Do - na no - bis pa - cem, Do - na, Do - na no-
us, Give us, Lord, en - dur - ing peace, give us, give us, Lord,

- na, Do - na no - bis pa - cem, Do - na, Do-na no - bis, pacem,
us, Give us, Lord, en - dur - ing peace, give us, Lord, en - dur - ing peace,

- na, Do - na no - bis pa - cem, Do - na, Do-na no - bis pa -
us, Give us, Lord, give us peace, give us, Lord, en - dur - ing peace,......

- na, Do - na no - bis pa - cem, Do - na, Do-na
us, Give us, Lord, en - dur - ing peace, give us, Give us,

TUTTI.
- bis pa - cem, no - bis pa - cem, Do - na no-bis, do - na
en - dur - ing peace, en - dur - ing peace, In thy ten - der care be-

TUTTI.
Do-na no - bis, no - bis pa - cem, Do - na no - bis, do - na
Give us, Lord, O give en - dur - ing peace, In thy ten - der care be-

TUTTI.
- cem, do - na no - bis, no - bis pa - cem, Do - na no - bis, do - na
.... en - dur - ing, give en - dur - ing peace,........ In thy ten - der care be-

TUTTI.
no - bis pa - cem, Do - na no - bis, no - bis pa - cem, Do - na no - bis, do - na
Lord, en - dur - ing peace, en - dur - ing peace, en - dur - ing peace, In thy care bestow re-

f

8vi.   8vi.

no - bis pa - cem,
stow relief from all our woe.

no - bis pa - cem.
stow relief from all our woe.

no - bis pa - cem.
stow relief from all our woe.

- lief from all our woe.

p

SOLI.
Do - na no - bis pa - cem, no - bis pa - cem,
Lord, thy mer - cies still increase, thy mercies increase,
SOLI.
Do - na no - bis pa - cem, no - bis pa - cem,
Lord, thy mer - cies still increase, thy mercies increase,
SOLI.
Do - na no - bis
Lord, thy mer - cies
SOLI.
p
Do - na no - bis pa - cem, Do - na no - bis pa -
Give us, Lord, en - dur - ing peace, en - dur - ing peace,
Do - na no - b's pa - cem, Do-na no-bis, no - bis pacem, pa -
Give us, Lord, en - dur - ing, Give us peace, give us peace, peace
pa - cem, Dona no - bis pa - cem, Dona no - bis pa - cem, no - bis
still increase, Give us, Lord, en - dur - ing peace, Give us peace, give us peace, give us, Lord, en -
pa - cem, Dona no - bis pa - cem, Dona no - bis pa - cem, pa -
still increase, Give us, Lord, en - dur - ing peace, Give us peace, give peace, O Lord,
TUTTI.
- cem, Do - na no - bis, no - bis pa - cem, Do -
Give us, give us Lord, en - dur - ing peace, Give
- cem, Do - na no - bis, no - bis pa - cem,
Give us, Lord, en - dur - ing peace.
TUTTI.
pa - cem, Do - na no - bis, no - bis pa - cem, Do - na
- dur - ing peace, Give us, Lord, en - dur-ing, en dur - ing peace, Give us,

- na no - - - bis pa - - - cem, pa - cem, Do - na no - bis, no - bis
us, Lord, en - dur - ing, en - dur - ing peace, In thy ten - der care, thy
Do-na nobis, nobis pacem, no - bis pa - cem, Do - na no - bis, no - bis
Lord, thy mercies still increase, Lord, thy mer - cies still increase, thy care be -
no - - bis pa - - cem, no - bis pa - cem, Do - na no - bis no - bis
Lord, en - dur - - ing peace, en - dur - ing peace, In thy ten - der care be -
no - - bis pa - - cem, pa - - cem, Do - na no - bis no - bis
Lord, en - dur - - ing peace, In thy ten - der care be -
8vi.
SOLI.
pa - - cem, Do - - na pa - - - cem,
care be - stow, Soli. In thy ten - - der care,
pa - - cem, Do - na no - bis pa - cem, pa - cem,
stow, Soli. In thy ten - der care be - stow, be - stow,
pa - - cem, Do - na no - bis pa - - cem, pa - cem,
- stow, In thy ten - der care be - stow re - lief from woe,
SOLI.
pa - - cem, no - bis pa - cem,
- stow, In thy care be - stow,
p
TUTTI.
Do - na no - bis, Do - - na no - bis pa - - cem no - bis pa - cem.
Full re - lief from all our woe, be - stow full re - lief.... from all.... our woe.
Do - na no - bis, Do - - na no - bis pa - - cem no - bis pa - cem.
Full re - lief from all our woe, be - stow full re - lief.... from all.... our woe.
TUTTI.
Do - na no - bis, Do - - na no - bis pa - - cem no - bis pa - cem.
Full re - lief from all our woe, be - stow full re - lief from all our woe.
TUTTI.
f

ET INCARNATUS. SOLO & CHORUS.

Owing to the extreme difficulty of the Incarnatus in this Mass, the following has been added, and may be substituted.

Adagio. SOLO. TENOR.

Et in-carnatus est, de spiritu sanc-to, ex Ma-ri-a Vir-gi-ne,
When Christ in Bethlehem took on him the form of man, of the Vir-gin's child,

SOLO. BASS.

Et in-carnatus est, de spiritu sanc-to, ex Ma-ri-a Vir-gi-ne,
When Christ in Bethlehem took on him the form of man, of the Vir-gin's child, dim.

Adagio.

p SOLO. TREBLE.

Et in-car-na-tus est, de spi-ritu sanc-to, ex Ma-ri-a Vir-gi-
When Christ in Bethlehem born, the Virgin's holy child, as the child of Ma-

Et in-car-na-tus est, de spi-ritu sanc-to, ex Ma-ri-a Vir-gi-
When Christ in Bethlehem born, the Virgin's holy child, as the child of Ma-

Et in-carnatus est de spi-ritu sanc-to, de spi-ri-tu sancto, ex Ma-ri-a Vir-gi-
When Christ in Bethlehem born, assumed our mortal state, he humbled himself to be the child of Ma-

Et in-car-natus est, et in-car-natus est, de spi-ri-tu sancto, ex Ma-ri-a Vir-gi-
When Christ in Bethlehem born, assumed our mortal state, He humbled himself to be the child of Ma-

-ne, ho-mo factus est, ho-mo fac-tus est, ho-mo, ho-mo
-ry, And became a man, and in mortal state, mor-tal, and in

-ne, ho-mo factus est, ho-mo fac-tus est, ho-mo, ho-mo
-ry, And became a man, and in mortal state, mor-tal, and in

-ne, ho-mo factus est, ho-mo fac-tus est, ho-mo, ho-mo
-ry, And became a man, and in mortal state, mor-tal, and in

-ne, Et ho-mo fac-tus est, et ho-mo factus est, et ho-mo, ho-mo
-ry, Became a man, became a man, to test our mor-tal state, and suf-fered

TUTTI.
ff
fac - tus est, Cru - ci - fix - us, Cru - ci -
mor - tal state, To re - deem us, To re -
fac - tus est, Cru - ci - fix - us, Cru - ci -
mor - tal state, To re - deem us, To re -
fac - tus est, Cru - ci - fix - us, Cru - ci -
mor - tal state, To re - deem us, To re -
fac - tus est, Cru - ci - fix - us, Cru - ci -
all...... our woes, To re - deem us, To re -
cres.
pp
- fix - us, e - ti - am pro no - bis, Pas - sus, pas - sus, pas - sus
- deem us, Cru - ci - fied to save us, Suf - fered, suf - fered, died and
et...... se - pul - tus est.
in...... the tomb was laid.